AMAZING STORIES OF SURVIVAL

Pamela Rushby

CONTENTS

DON'T PANIC!

Sometimes, people find themselves in very dangerous situations. Someone could be stranded in a scorching desert, lost on a snow-covered mountain, or even trapped in a collapsed mine. It can seem impossible to survive in situations like these, when a single decision might mean the difference between life and death.

It is vital to be prepared in case something goes wrong, but the most important thing is not to panic when faced with danger. Survival experts say that fear and panic can stop people from thinking clearly, which makes it difficult to plan an escape from a **perilous** situation.

When somebody is in a dangerous situation, survival experts suggest they stop, sit down, think through the situation, and consider the following:

- What do I have that could help me to survive?
- What can I do to assist rescuers who may be on their way?
- Is there any shelter, warmth, food, and water?
- Is it possible to signal to rescuers?

The people in this book were trapped, or lost, in different ways. Their reactions were all very different. These are the stories of the decisions they made and how they survived.

STRANDED IN THE DESERT

People looking for a real four-wheel-drive challenge often consider driving the Canning Stock Route in Western Australia. It has been called one of the greatest four-wheel-drive adventures in the world.

The Canning Stock Route is a track that runs from Halls Creek, in the Kimberley region, to Wiluna, in the Midwest region. The route was first used in 1910 by **cowboys** moving their cattle across the state. Today, it is about 1,180 miles of rough trails through the desert and over sand dunes, with only the occasional well for water.

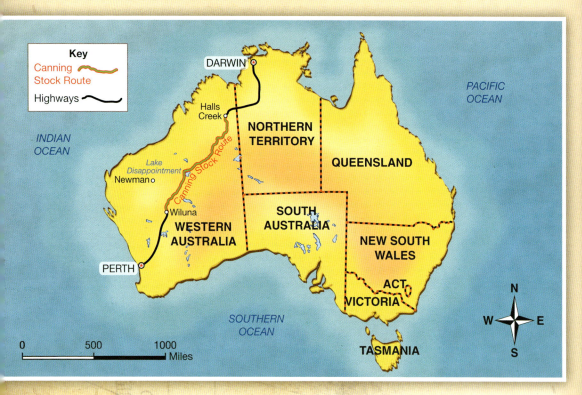

The Canning Stock Route connects Wiluna and Halls Creek in Western Australia.

Driving the Canning Stock Route takes between two and three weeks, and four-wheel-drive **enthusiasts** have to plan very carefully before they set out. They usually travel in a **convoy** during the cooler months of the year, and their vehicles are well maintained and stocked with food, water, spare tires, and communication devices. Fuel supplies need to be arranged in advance, as there is nowhere to buy gas in the desert.

CANNING STOCK ROUTE
This road is recommended for
4WD vehicles only

There is no water, fuel or services
between Wiluna and Halls Creek,
over 1900km in length
ATS4X4.COM
Motorists are advised to obtain
adequate supplies and spares before
venturing on this road

There are signs at the start of the Canning Stock Route to warn travelers of the dangers.

In October 2002, a 36-year-old German tourist named Kim Hardt set out alone on the Canning Stock Route. He had seen a documentary about the route on television in Germany and thought it seemed like a challenging, exciting adventure.

It can be dangerous to drive the Canning Stock Route alone.

At home in Germany, Kim bought a map of the Canning Stock Route. He traveled to Australia and rented a sports utility vehicle (SUV). He departed from Wiluna in Western Australia, aiming for Darwin in the Northern Territory. He did not tell anyone where he was planning to go, and he set out on the Canning Stock Route by himself, expecting to drive it in two or three days. He had no phone or **GPS equipment**, and only a small amount of food and water.

About 370 miles into his journey, Kim's vehicle got stuck in the mud on the shore of Lake Disappointment, 250 miles east of Newman. By this time, he had only a box of cookies and two pints of water left.

Three days later, his luck changed. He was very fortunate to be spotted by a passing group of tourists. They were unable to release his vehicle, so they left him with some extra water and set off to find a rescue team. By the time the helicopter arrived to airlift him to safety, Kim had been reduced to drinking the salty water from Lake Disappointment.

Desert survival experts said that Kim did the right thing by staying with his vehicle until he was found. If he had wandered away from the vehicle, he might never have been seen again.

Lake Disappointment appears white because of its high salt content.

LOST ON A FREEZING MOUNTAIN

On New Year's Eve in 2010, 14-year-old Jake Denham set out for a day's skiing with his family and some friends on Mount Bachelor in Oregon. It was a cold day, but the snow was perfect for skiing. Everyone was having a good time until Jake lost one of his skis. Rather than stay with his family and friends, Jake began looking for his ski in the snow.

Mount Bachelor is in the Cascade Range in central Oregon.

When he could not locate his ski, Jake decided to take off his remaining ski and walk down the mountain. He didn't know the way, but he thought that if he kept walking downhill, he would come across a trail. He set off, stumbling through the deep snow.

It began to grow dark, and the temperature dropped lower and lower.

Jake was skiing on Mount Bachelor when he lost sight of his family and friends.

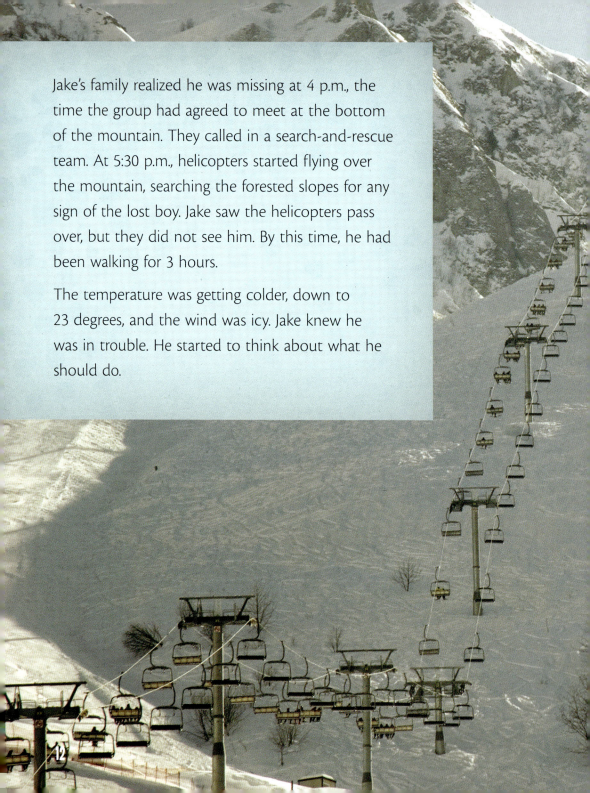

Jake's family realized he was missing at 4 p.m., the time the group had agreed to meet at the bottom of the mountain. They called in a search-and-rescue team. At 5:30 p.m., helicopters started flying over the mountain, searching the forested slopes for any sign of the lost boy. Jake saw the helicopters pass over, but they did not see him. By this time, he had been walking for 3 hours.

The temperature was getting colder, down to 23 degrees, and the wind was icy. Jake knew he was in trouble. He started to think about what he should do.

Helicopters are often used by search-and-rescue teams to search over a large area.

Jake recalled some television shows he had watched, about people surviving in the wild. He realized that what he needed was shelter from the cold and the wind. He remembered how people on the television shows had built shelters. He started to dig in the snow, making a small cave where he could huddle away from the wind. Jake stayed there for several hours. His outer clothes were icy, and his gloves had frozen solid. Jake began to wonder if his snow cave was enough to save him. But he was determined to get out of this situation.

Jake remembered another survival technique he had seen on television. He looked up at the sky and located the North Star, which is always in the north. That gave him some idea of which way to go, so he left his shelter and started downhill again. This time, Jake found something to follow: ski tracks. If he followed those, Jake reasoned, they would lead him down and off the mountain. He followed them, sometimes falling over and then searching on his hands and knees until he found the tracks again. It was midnight by now and getting even colder.

Even in the dark, Jake was able to follow ski tracks down the mountain.

Finally, far below him on the mountain, Jake saw lights. It was a search team. Jake was very cold and very hungry, but he was safe.

Later, Jake told news reporters how he had learned his survival skills from his favorite television shows. But, he added, he had learned two more things now: always ski with a buddy, and always eat a really good meal before going out on a mountain.

Jake was very lucky to survive in the cold for as long as he did.

BURIED DEEP UNDERGROUND

AN EARTHQUAKE

On April 25, 2006, an earthquake hit the town of Beaconsfield on the northern coast of Tasmania. The earthquake measured 2.3 on the **Richter scale**, which put it below "minor" on the scale. This means an earthquake that may not even be felt by humans but that can be recorded by a **seismograph**.

In Beaconsfield, the small earthquake had a very serious consequence. It caused an underground rockfall in the Beaconsfield gold mine.

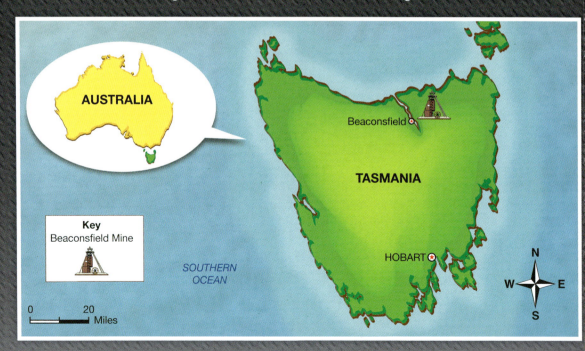

Beaconsfield is a mining town in the north of Tasmania.

Sadly, one miner, Larry Knight, was killed when the mine collapsed. The 14 other miners who were working underground at the time escaped from the mine. But two miners, Brant Webb and Todd Russell, were trapped underground by the rockfall. They were in the collapsed mine for 14 days before anyone was able to reach them.

The Beaconsfield gold mine was established in 1879.

At first, it was impossible to tell if the missing miners were safe. Immediately, heat-sensing cameras were lowered into the mine, searching for signs of body heat, which would tell rescuers that the men were alive. No one was very hopeful.

Brant and Todd *were* alive, but they were totally trapped. In fact, they could hardly move. When the mine collapsed, they had been working from inside a metal mesh cage on the long arm of a vehicle called a **teleloader**.

Brant and Todd were working from a teleloader cage when the mine collapsed.

When the earthquake struck, the rock around the teleloader collapsed into chunks of rubble. Once everything had settled down, Brant and Todd found that the cage had saved them. But it was partially filled with rock, and the two men were half-buried in the rubble. The crushed cage was over half a mile below the surface.

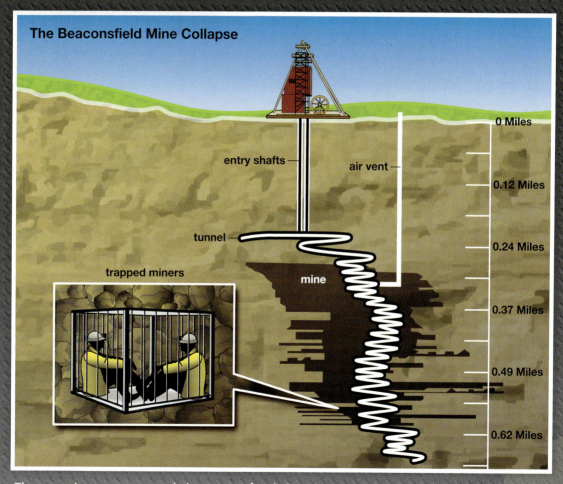

The Beaconsfield Mine Collapse

entry shafts

air vent

tunnel

trapped miners

mine

0 Miles

0.12 Miles

0.24 Miles

0.37 Miles

0.49 Miles

0.62 Miles

The two miners were trapped about 3,000 feet below the ground.

The space the two men occupied was about as wide as a single bed but not quite as long. They could not lie flat on their backs at the same time. One man had to always be on his side, and his shoulder would then touch the rocks above them. It was a very bad situation to be in.

Brant and Todd began to assess their situation. They had one tool —a **utility knife**—and they were able to use this to cut through clothing and boots to free themselves from rubble.

Brant also had a muesli bar, which the two men agreed to share. They had no idea how long it would have to last, so they finally began to eat it on April 29, 4 days after the rockfall. To make the bar last as long as possible, they ate very small pieces.

They were able to drink **groundwater** that seeped through the rocks above them, collecting it in a helmet.

The men waited and waited each trying to reassure the other that rescuers were looking for them and that they would be found. They were **determined** to survive.

This re-enactment shows that the teleloader cage was too small for the miners to both lie on their backs.

THE RESCUE

Five days after the earthquake, the heat-sensing cameras showed that there were people still alive in the mine. On April 30, the rescuers located the two men, though they could not reach them. They passed a microphone through the rubble, so they could speak to the trapped miners.

The rockfall made it very difficult for rescuers to reach the trapped miners.

Brant and Todd had been found, but it was another nine days before they were able to leave the mine. In the meantime, the rescuers passed a 40-foot-long plastic tube through the rubble. Water, blankets, and glow sticks for light were sent along the tube, followed by food, a camera, medical supplies, and messages from Brant's and Todd's families.

Then the rescuers slowly started to move the unstable rock rubble. They had to construct a new tunnel for the rescue because the old one was unsafe.

The rescue team worked six-hour shifts, crouching in a tunnel only three-feet wide. They were forced to work on their knees, operating a drill. The work was exhausting, as they had to fully support the weight of the heavy drill as they cleared the rock above them.

Journalists and camerapeople from all over Australia came to Beaconsfield to report on the rescue.

When they knew they were getting closer, the rescue team began clearing loose rock and gravel. They were securing the area with concrete to stop more rockfalls from occurring.

Media had arrived from all around the country, sending out reports on the rescue. Soon, it seemed that all of Australia was following the rescue attempt on radio, television, and in the newspapers.

Finally, at 4:27 a.m. on May 9, a rescue party broke through the last of the rubble separating them from the two miners. They shouted that they could see the miners' light, and Brant and Todd replied that they could see the lights of the rescue party. It seemed like a miracle.

Glenn Burns was the first rescuer to reach the trapped miners. He used a crowbar to chip his way through the last of the rocks. He said afterwards, "Suddenly, through the crack, I could see Todd's eye looking at me like a little possum. I made the crack bigger, stuck my hand through, and shook their hands."

The teleloader cage full of rubble from the rockfall has been reconstructed at the Beaconsfield Mine & Heritage Center.

The rescuers found that the two men had shared body heat and used one of their helmets as a toilet. When the team saw the cage and all the rocks around the men, they found it very hard to understand how Brant and Todd had survived.

Early that morning, Beaconsfield heard the sound of a church bell ringing. The men were coming out of the mine! They were taken to the hospital immediately to be examined after their ordeal. They had been buried for 14 days.

Todd Russell (left) and Brant Webb (center) walked free from the Beaconsfield gold mine after 14 days underground.

A book was written about the amazing survival of the two miners, and a television miniseries was produced. Today, at the Beaconsfield Mine & Heritage Center, visitors to the Mine Rescue exhibition can experience how it might have felt to be trapped underground for 14 days—including a **multisensory simulation** of the earthquake and rockfall.

The book about the rescue, *Bad Ground*, was written by journalist Tony Wright.

DETERMINED TO SURVIVE

So how did the people in these three situations manage to live?

Kim Hardt had done little planning for his drive. As a result, he did not have enough food and water, and he did not understand the harshness of the country he was attempting to cross. But when he found himself in trouble, he did not panic. He stayed in one place and hoped for rescue. He was very fortunate help came when it did.

Jake Denham learned that it is always wise to ski with a buddy. When he found himself in trouble, however, he stopped and thought about his situation. He used what he had learned from television shows to understand he needed shelter and then plotted a way to find a route down the mountain.

Brant Webb and Todd Russell had to plan how to survive until rescue teams found them. They collected water, rationed out their food, and used what tools they had to free themselves from rubble.

These people were in very different, very dangerous situations. But each of them kept calm and thought through their **predicament**. And they had one thing in common—they were determined to survive.

GLOSSARY

convoy (*noun*) a group of vehicles traveling together

determined (*adjective*) decided, certain

enthusiasts (*noun*) people with a strong common interest

GPS equipment (*noun*) Global Positioning System equipment; devices that show a person exactly where they are located

groundwater (*noun*) surface water that has seeped below ground

multisensory simulation (*noun*) a re-creation of an event using senses such as sight, hearing, touch, and smell

perilous (*adjective*) dangerous or full of risk

predicament (*noun*) an unpleasant, difficult situation

Richter scale (*noun*) the scale used to measure the total energy of an earthquake

seismograph (*noun*) an instrument for measuring and recording earthquakes

teleloader (*noun*) a vehicle used to reach high places

utility knife (*noun*) a tool with a sharp blade that is pushed out to cut things

INDEX